PARABHAKTI

by
Nome

Published by
Society of Abidance in Truth (SAT)
1834 Ocean Street
Santa Cruz, CA 95060   USA
(831) 425-7287
web: www.SATRamana.org
email: sat@cruzio.com

CONTENTS

OM NAMO BHAGAVATE
SRI RAMANAYA

ACKNOWLEDGEMENTS

Gratitude is expressed here for the proofreading effort of Raymond Teague. Appreciation is also here expressed to Sasvati for the layout and design of this book and seeing to the printing of it. Finally, deep appreciation is expressed to those devotees at the SAT Temple who, through their dedication and offerings, enable SAT to continue to make the teachings of nondual Self-Knowledge available to seekers of Truth.

Introduction

Presented here are writings by Nome, preceded by quotes from Sri Ramana Maharshi and Sri Adi Sankara. They are an offering to Lord Siva, to Sadguru Ramana, and to all sages of the lineage of Advaita Vedanta.

Upon reading this little book, the reader immediately will recognize that he or she is reading writings of both a devotional nature and writings expressive of jnana—Knowledge. This is Parabhakti—supreme devotion.

The first part of this book is in seven chapters. The reader will note subtle differences among the chapters. The first and second chapters describe bhakti (devotion), while the third chapter describes the experience of the bhakta (devotee). The fourth chapter takes the bhakta deeper into jnana through the relationship with the Guru, while the fifth chapter speaks of continuous, absorbing devotion to God and Guru. The sixth describes the practice of the bhakta and the spiritual activities and attitudes with which a bhakta infuses his or her life, and the seventh describes absorption, through bhakti, in jnana.

The second part of this book is in six chapters consisting of a collection of poetry. Chapter I, *Namah Sivaya*, presents short verses praising Lord Siva, while simultaneously expressing Knowledge of the Lord.

Chapter II, *In Praise of the One Like Space*, is a poem that is descriptive of Absolute Being and praising that Absolute.

Chapter III, *Realize the One Like Space*, is composed of verses that pose questions that, if asked, guide the bhakta to realize the One like space.

Chapter IV, *Space of Grace*, is a set of verses descriptive of the One like space—a description of Grace.

Chapter V, *Within the One Like Space*, features verses describing the experience of the space that is the One Absolute.

Chapter VI, *Gracious Inquiry*, appears as both a solicitation for Grace and also

Knowledge of the ever-presence of Grace through inquiry.

Sri Bhagavan expresses His supreme devotion to His "Father"—the Lord—in His letter to His family when he left His uncle's house, "...*In search of my Father and in obedience to his command, I have started from here...*" He also expresses the same supreme devotion to Arunachala in many of His writings.

Adi Sankara tells us: *"The sense of non-duality may apply to the three worlds, but it is not to be used toward the Guru."*

Nome tells us: *"The joy of the disciple consists in his unimportance and nonexistence, while the sole existence and all-importance of his Guru is his nondual Bliss."*

These three powerhouses of Knowledge do not suggest an iota of dualism in what they express. Bhakti is jnana, and jnana is bhakti. One cannot exist without the other.

If a person practices pure, ego-less jnana, bhakti is unavoidable. On the other hand, if a person practices pure, ego-less bhakti, jnana is surely inevitable.

The glorious, lofty heights of devotion—jnana—are expressed here in this little book, and the sages assure us that the identical experience is available to all. It is sincerely hoped that the reader experiences the vastness of parabhakti while deeply meditating on these writings and remains absorbed therein.

Om Namah Sivaya
Sasvati

मोक्षकारणसामग्र्यां भक्तिरेव
गरीयसी ।
स्वस्वरूपानुसन्धानं
भक्तिरित्यभिधीयते ॥
स्वात्मतत्त्वानुसन्धानं
भक्तिरित्यपरे जगुः ॥

mokṣakāraṇasāmagryāṁ bhaktireva
garīyasī |
svasvarūpānusandhānaṁ bhaktir-
ityabhidhīyate ||
svātmatattvānusandhānaṁ bhaktir-
ityapare jaguḥ ||

mokṣakāraṇa = cause of/means to
    Liberation
sāmagryāṁ = completeness, totality, a
    means for
bhaktireva = devotion indeed
garīyasī = extremely important, dearer than,
    more valuable than, greater than
svasvarūpa = one's own true nature
anusandhānaṁ = investigation, inquiry
bhaktirityabhidhīyate = devotion thus
    considered
svātmatattvā = one's Self Truth
ānusandhānaṁ = investigation, inquiry
bhaktiriti = devotion thus
apare = in another, in/on having nothing
    beyond/superior
 jaguḥ = they sang

The completeness of the means for Liberation, devotion (bhakti), indeed, is extremely important (great, dear, valuable). Inquiry into (investigation of) one's own true nature is thus considered bhakti. "Inquiry into the Truth of one's Self is bhakti," thus, in another [scriptural passage], they sang.

✦

from Maharshi's Gospel
by Sri Ramana Maharshi

The Guru is the Self. Sometime in his life, man becomes dissatisfied with it, and, not content with what he has, he seeks the satisfaction of his desires through prayer to God etc. His mind is gradually purified until he longs to know God more to obtain His Grace than to satisfy his worldly desires. Then, God's Grace begins to manifest. God takes the form of a Guru and appears to the devotee, teaches him the Truth, and, moreover, purifies his mind by association. The devotee's mind gains strength and is then able to turn inward. By meditation, it is further purified, and it remains still without the least ripple. That calm expanse is the Self.

The Guru is both "external" and "internal." From the "exterior," He gives a push to the mind to turn inward; from the "interior," He pulls the mind toward the Self and helps in the quieting of the mind. That is Guru-kripa. There is no difference between God, Guru, and the Self.

The Master is within. Meditation is meant to remove the ignorant idea that

He is only outside. If He be a stranger whom you await, He is bound to disappear also. Where is the use for a transient being like that? But, as long as you think that you are separate or that you are the body, so long is the Master "without" also necessary, and He will appear as if with a body. When the wrong identification of oneself with the body ceases, the Master will be found as none other than the Self.

Does the Guru hold you by the hand and whisper in the ear? You may imagine him to be what you are yourself. Because you think that you are with a body, you think that He also has a body to do something tangible to you. His work lies within, in the spiritual realm.

God, who is immanent, in His Grace, takes pity on the loving devotee and manifests Himself according to the devotee's development. The devotee thinks that He is a man and expects a relationship as between two physical bodies. But the Guru, who is God or the Self incarnate, works from within, helps the man to see the error of his ways, and guides him in the right path until he realizes the Self within.

D.: What should the devotee do then?

M.: He has only to accept the words

of the Master and work within. The Master is both "within" and "without," so He creates conditions to drive you inward and, at the same time, prepares the "interior" to drag you to the center. Thus, He gives a push from "without" and exerts a pull from "within," so that you may be fixed at the center.

You think that the world can be conquered by your own efforts. When you are frustrated externally and are driven inward, you feel, "Oh! There is a power higher than man!"

The ego is like a very powerful elephant that cannot be brought under control by any less powerful than a lion, which, in this instance, is no other than the Guru, whose very look makes the elephant-like ego tremble and die.

You will know in due course that your glory lies where you cease to exist. In order to gain that state, you should surrender yourself. Then, the Master sees that you are in a fit state to receive guidance, and He guides you.

Silence is the most potent form of work. However vast and emphatic the Scriptures may be, they fail in their effect. The Guru is silent, and Grace prevails in *all. This Silence is vaster and more emphatic than all the Scriptures put together.*

The devotee surrenders himself to the Master, and it means that there is no vestige of individuality retained by him. If the surrender is complete, all sense of self is lost, and then there can be no misery or sorrow.

The eternal Being is nothing but Happiness. That comes as a revelation.

Grace is the Self. That also is not to be acquired; you need only to know that it exists. The sun is brightness only. It does not see darkness. Yet, you speak of darkness fleeing on the sun's approach. So, also, the devotee's ignorance, like the phantom of darkness, vanishes at the look of the Guru. You are surrounded by sunlight, yet, if you would see the sun, you must turn in its direction and look at it. So, also, Grace is found by the proper approach you make, though it is here and now.

Leave it all to the Master. Surrender to Him without reserve. One of two things must be done: either surrender yourself, because you realize your inability and need a Higher Power to help you or in-

vestigate into the cause of misery, go into the Source, and so merge in (with) the Self. Either way, you will be free from misery. God or Guru never forsakes the devotee who has surrendered himself.

Inasmuch as there is no ego in the sage, there are no "others" for him. What is the highest benefit that can be conferred on you? It is happiness, and happiness is born of peace. Peace can reign only where there is no disturbance, and disturbance is due to thoughts that arise in the mind. When the mind itself is absent, there will be perfect peace. Unless a person has annihilated the mind, he cannot gain peace and be happy. And unless he himself be happy, he cannot bestow happiness on "others." Since, however, there are no "others" for the sage who has no mind, the mere fact of His Self-realization is itself enough to make the "others" happy.

✦

from Origin of Spiritual Instruction
by Sri Ramana Maharshi

The Supreme Lord is eternal Grace itself. Therefore, there is really no such individual act as the showering of His Grace, and, being ever present, the manifestation of Grace is not confined to any particular period or occasion.

The Scriptures declare that, for the sake of the aspirant, who, seeking true Knowledge and Enlightenment, in other words to realize the Supreme, is devoted to the Lord with no desire but to attain His Grace, that Divinity, which is really the core of his being and is ever present in him as pure Consciousness, the Seer of sight, takes up, at the right time, as a result of such devotion and out of solicitude for him, a human form of the three-fold inherent qualities of Sat-Chit-Ananda and appears before him as the Master. Further, the scriptures state explicitly that, through his Grace, the Master helps and enables the disciple to lose himself utterly in and become even as, or identical with, his Master. The Master should, therefore, be recognized as none other than the Supreme Being.

✦

from Sri Ramana Gita, Chapter 16 by Sri Ramana Maharshi

2. The Self is dear to all. Nothing else is as dear as the Self. Love, unbroken like a stream of oil, is termed bhakti.

3. Through love, the Sage knows that God is none other than his own Self. Though the devotee, on the other hand, regards Him as different from himself, yet he, too, dissolves and abides in the Self alone.

8. When bhakti has grown perfect, then, hearing once (about Reality) is enough, for it confers perfect Knowledge.

9. Bhakti not continuous like a stream is called intermittent bhakti. Even this is bound to result in supreme bhakti.

10. One who practices bhakti for a desired end finds no fulfillment on attaining it and then again worships God for the sake of eternal happiness.

12. Growing thus, bhakti, in the course of time, will become perfect. By means of this perfect, supreme bhakti, even as by jnana, one shall cross (the ocean of) becoming.

✦

from Origin of Spiritual Instruction
by Sri Ramana Maharshi

He is entirely free from the sense of "I" (ahamkara) and "mine" (mamakara), no matter what his body may appear to do or what he may appear to possess. He thus shines in the resplendent glory of selfless Existence. This, indeed, is what is called Parabhakti, or Supreme Devotion…

✦

PARABHAKTI
PART I

Chapter I

That which exists and reveals itself as God and Guru is the Supreme, the One Absolute. To love That as none other than the Self is supreme devotion to the Supreme, or parabhakti.

✦

Abidance free of the ego-notion, devoid of the delusive concepts of "I" and "mine," is bhakti.

✦

Being full of faith that remains unwavering is bhakti.

✦

Reverence for the sacred, with natural humility, is bhakti.

✦

Complete, invariable, deep, unshakable
trust in God or Guru is bhakti.

✦

Continuous love of the Supreme, for the
sake of that One alone, is bhakti.

✦

Gratitude toward the source of all the
good that manifests, remaining unmoved
by all that appears otherwise, and being
completely detached from worldly
concerns is bhakti.

✦

To be ever at peace and free of the least
trace of self-concern, wholly introspective,
and not imagining happiness to be
dependent upon others but being
completely certain that the Supreme is
happiness itself, is bhakti.

✦

Gladness for any sacred opportunity,
joyful worship, happy immersion in

*meditation without difference, and
absorption in the supreme bliss of
Knowledge of the true Self is bhakti.*

✦

*To hold the teachings received as most
precious, their source with reverence and
love, having full faith in them and in the
source, constantly endeavoring to abide in
the truth of them, listening to them,
reflecting upon them, continuously deeply
meditating upon them, and remaining
absorbed in the truth of them, finding
delight therein, is bhakti.*

✦

*To remain ever-thankful for the spiritual
instruction received that reveals the Truth
and awakens from delusion, keenly
aware of the immeasurable immensity
of Grace, is bhakti.*

✦

*Dedication of all the activities and the
instruments of action, body, speech, and*

13

mind, to the Supreme, while being free of the idea of being a performer of action and free of misidentification with those instruments, is bhakti.

✦

Freedom from ignorance because of the essential Knowledge inherent in bhakti, freedom from desire because of the illimitable, boundless bliss inwardly revealed by bhakti, and freedom from anger because of deep peace born of the indestructibility of bhakti are the characteristics of the realization of the Supreme, and such is bhakti.

✦

The manifestation of qualities that are true, good, and beautiful, while yet not conceiving oneself as in possession of any qualities, manifesting that which is divine, while entirely free of the ideas of manifestation and an individual to do so, and remaining as that which is forever without birth or creation, is bhakti.

✦

To surrender all, including the idea of oneself, to the Supreme One, even in the midst of the application of effort, knowing that this Supreme One, the One worthy of worship, alone is to be surrendered to, the One that absorbs all, destroying the notions of "I" and "this," is bhakti.

✦

Surrendering so as to abide free of attachment and anxious thought, even when in the midst of giving sustained, careful attention to the offered activity, is bhakti.

✦

Dedication of the entirety of what constitutes this life to the Supreme and constant meditation on that divine One is bhakti.

✦

Offering with a sincere heart full of love is bhakti.

✦

Perception of the worthlessness, smallness, powerlessness, insignificance, and nonexistence of the ego in the light of the knowledge of the Supreme One as the true treasure, the infinite and omnipresent, the omnipotent, the all-important Reality, and the ever-existent true Being of the Self is bhakti.

✦

The effacement of the ego is bhakti.

✦

Freedom from the mistaken conception of "my" in relation to any mind, body, or object, and remaining joyful in the One to whom all belong is bhakti.

✦

Trusting in that One, relying utterly upon that One, seeking refuge in that One, finding joy in that One, loving that One, dwelling in the peace of that One, and being ever absorbed in that One, as that One, is bhakti.

✦

Knowing with certainty that the bhakta never perishes, identified with that to which one is devoted, which is eternal, and abidance in a state of continuous, difference-less devotion is bhakti.

✦

Dissolution of the forms of the mind by the power of devotion, believing in the Divine more than any idea conjured in the mind, attracting the mind to its dissolution by the joyful love of the inner bliss, is bhakti.

✦

To remain in awe of the infinite and eternal, yet free of the misconception of separation, with the ego notion gone and the mind transcended, is bhakti.

✦

To abide unmoving, without giving rise to illusion, free of attachment to the transient unreality, desireless and fearless, absorbed by the power of devotion that gives birth to Knowledge, in That, as That, is bhakti.

✦

Invariable abidance in That from which the universe appears, by which it appears, in which it appears, for which it appears, whose it is, into which it disappears, by which it disappears, for which it disappears, and which it truly is, is bhakti.

✦

Worshiping that One, contemplating upon that One, speaking of that One, singing about that One, hearing about that One, listening to that One, reading about that One, meditating on that One, inquiring to realize that One, and abiding in That, as That, is bhakti.

✦

*To know that all is within and by that
Supreme One, yet free of the idea of
destiny, and to know that Supreme One
to be the Self, yet free of the idea of
free will, is bhakti.*

✦

*Knowing that Grace, limitless and
always, is ever the one existent power,
with reliance on that for all things and
purposes, desirous of nothing but to
remain ever aware of that Grace,
is bhakti.*

✦

*To abide unaffected, blissful and peaceful
without suffering, by any occurrence,
because of complete devotion is bhakti.*

✦

*Loving God or Guru in one's fellow
bhaktas, knowing such to be their true
Self, shining in the luminous joy of such,*

*remaining One with That, transcendent
of their illusory attributes, is bhakti.*

✦

*Complete love of the Supreme, loving all
in the knowledge of the Supreme as their
very Self, transcendent of action, word, or
thought, and loving this Self as one's Self,
as the only Self, is bhakti.*

✦

*Meditation in wonder and awe on the
vast, verily infinite, nature of the eternal
Supreme One and absorption in That
is bhakti.*

✦

*Immersion in bliss, having forgotten how
to suffer and be sorrowful, having
abandoned the concerns of the ego, and
losing the false supposition of
individuality, is bhakti.*

✦

*Other-less devotion, with all dualism
gone, the Supreme Lord one's only*

*identity, remaining in firm devotion to
that one Self who alone eternally exists,
is bhakti.*

✦

*Merger with the Supreme, in undivided
devotion that reveals that nonduality is
truth, forsaking the false assumption of a
separate individuality and all of its
attributes, is bhakti.*

✦

*Abidance as That, the Supreme One,
which is all, which is beyond all, which is
entirely free of even a trace of all, which is
within all, which is not within anything
else whatsoever; in which all are, yet in
which nothing else is, the One without
a second, is bhakti.*

✦

*To know God with God's Knowledge of
God, and not by the jiva's (the
individual's) conception,
is bhakti.*

✦

*Love of God to such an extent and to such
a depth that nothing exists but God
is bhakti.*

✦

*Devotion to the Guru to such an extent
and to such a depth that the very Being
of the Guru is all that remains of one's
identity, the Existence of the Self,
is bhakti.*

✦

*Absorption of one's very identity in the
Self, Brahman, is pure bhakti. Beyond
description is parabhakti.*

✦

*In the Temple of Being,
The Space of Consciousness,*

ॐ श्री रमणार्पणमस्तु

om śrī ramaṇārpaṇamastu

*Om. May this be an offering to
Sri Ramana*

Chapter II

Bhakti is the certainty of the Knowledge of the Self in the state of identity with that.

✦

Bhakti is the dissolution of the illusion of identity as a separate self.

✦

Bhakti is the liberating absorption of one's sense of identity in that to which one is devoted.

✦

Bhakti is the blissful absorption that reveals happiness to be natural and renders suffering impossible.

✦

Bhakti is the means to itself.

✦

Bhakti is the faith of the bhakta (devotee), the cause of the humility of the bhakta, the freedom of the bhakta, the fearlessness of the bhakta, the peace of the bhakta, the love of the bhakta, the spiritual glory of the bhakta, and the very Self of the bhakta.

✦

Bhakti is the devotion in which and by which the devotee loses all belief in an ego-notion and no longer has even the least interest in any thought that pertains to that false identity.

✦

Bhakti is the sublime freedom from misidentification with a body and a mind and as the possessor of them, knowing that they belong to the One to whom one is devoted.

✦

Bhakti is identification only with the infinite, eternal One, for any other identity is due only to weakness of devotion, which is actually the weakness of

ignorance, as devotion is always pure
and flawless.

✦

Bhakti is the disappearance of the illusion
of differences in the realization of the
undifferentiated, omnipresent, unmodified
One, so that this One remains completely
one's Self with no scope for separation
or distinction.

✦

Bhakti is that which makes known the
inconceivable, reveals the imperceptible,
and bestows direct experience of the
all-transcendent God.

✦

Bhakti is that which yields perfect peace
free of birth and death by means of
absorption in that in which one
is simply, only That.

✦

Bhakti is the love of one's Self,
God's love of God.

✦

Bhakti is that by which one knows God
as God knows God, and no separate
knower or known remains.

✦

Bhakti is abidance as God as God is, and
as God alone is.

✦

Parabhakti is beyond conception.

✦

In the Temple of Being,
The Space of Consciousness,

ॐ श्री रमणार्पणमस्तु

om śrī ramaṇārpaṇamastu

Om. May this be an offering to
Sri Ramana

✦

Chapter III

A bhakta is a jnani, and a jnani is a bhakta.

✦

A bhakta loves God, knows what is loved, becomes what is known, and truly is that.

✦

A bhakta knows that which makes the ego inconsequential and nonexistent, and upon this rests the bhakta's profound humility and consistent transcendence.

✦

A bhakta's body is a temple, a servant, and an instrument, and the bhakta knows it as such, but the Self of the bhakta is not a body and knows that as such.

✦

A bhakta is the Self of all beings, and thus, with this knowledge, is the bhakta's love for all beings.

✦

A bhakta's devotion endows the bhakta with such matchless happiness that desire and fear can no longer be imagined, and thus the bhakta comes to know the unimaginable Bliss of the Supreme One.

✦

A bhakta can never be separated from bhakti and, thus, from God and Guru, and, by bhakti, the bhakta rests securely in this divine knowledge.

✦

A bhakta knows the Knowledge of the Knower, which is the Knowledge of the knowers, ignores the ignorance of the ignorant, and, seeing the true, remains true in bhakti.

✦

A bhakta is the identity by which one passes beyond all false definitions to realize the Knowledge of the Supreme

*Self, in which the bhakta's divinity is
rooted and abides.*

✦

*A bhakta sees God, who is One without a
second and forever immutable, alone as
all this and knows that the supposed
other-than-God has neither substance nor
power, neither creation nor existence.*

✦

*Parabhakti is complete absorption of
the bhakta.*

✦

*In the Temple of Being,
The Space of Consciousness,*

ॐ श्री रमणार्पणमस्तु

om śrī ramaṇārpaṇamastu

*Om. May this be an offering to
Sri Ramana*

✦

Chapter IV

In bhakti is found the answer to the question, the solution to the problem, the end of the turmoil and suffering of samsara, the disappearance of the anguish and confusion of the mind, and the peace that is imperishable.

✦

In bhakti is found the recognition of who, in truth, the Guru is.

✦

In bhakti is realized the profundity of the Guru's silence.

✦

In bhakti lies the ability to comprehend the Guru's spiritual instruction and the capacity to adhere to it.

✦

In bhakti is experienced the reality of Grace, which is omnipotent.

✦

In bhakti, the Guru is always present in the bhakta's heart, shining with deep peace and the revelation of Knowledge that transcends the world and the mind.

✦

In bhakti, the bhakta is united with the Guru with a love that is indestructible and that precludes separation.

✦

In bhakti, by the grace and spiritual instruction of the Guru, the bhakta finds that the seemingly solid illusion has disappeared and the seemingly etheric, mysterious Absolute is solidly real and self-evident.

✦

In bhakti, the Guru is realized to be completely the Self, and the misidentification as an ego is utterly lost.

✦

*In bhakti, worship becomes illumined,
meditation continuous, the symbols alive,
the temple one's home, the scriptures'
meaning open, devoted service the activity
of the divine, happiness full, peace
complete, and love reaches its zenith as,
by Self-Knowledge, the eternal Existence
of God is realized as one's own.*

✦

*In bhakti that is like a river, an unbroken
current, the bhakta reaches the shoreless,
fathomless ocean of Being-Consciousness-
Bliss by dissolution and remains
absorbed therein.*

✦

Parabhakti is the perfectly full perfection.

✦

*In the Temple of Being,
The Space of Consciousness,*

ॐ श्री रमणार्पणमस्तु

om śrī ramaṇārpaṇamastu

*Om. May this be an offering to
Sri Ramana*

◆

Chapter V

*To abide in the Knowledge of the Truth,
free of wavering and ignorance, is ceaseless bhakti.*

◆

*To remain fully in the supreme bliss,
free of disturbance and suffering, is
ceaseless bhakti.*

◆

*The devotion to the Guru, ever filled with
gratitude and always aware of the Guru's
grace, is ceaseless bhakti.*

◆

*The unending love of God for the very
Existence of God, is ceaseless bhakti.*

✦

The eternal love for the Eternal is
ceaseless bhakti.

✦

The undiminishing adherence to the
spiritual instruction that reveals the
Supreme One is ceaseless bhakti.

✦

Devotion that makes use of all
circumstances and experiences to further
deepen that devotion is ceaseless bhakti.

✦

Devotion that encompasses and pervades
the entirety of life, united with the
knowledge that the Supreme One alone
is the Reality, survives death and is
ceaseless bhakti.

✦

The devotion to the Supreme One that
brings peaceful transcendence of all and

yields identification with that eternal One is ceaseless bhakti.

✦

To remain beyond the states of mind, beyond the conditions of the body, untouched by thought and unchanged by sensation, and ever abiding in the Knowledge of That, by the Light of That, is ceaseless bhakti.

✦

The unbroken yearning for oneness with God by which one lifts oneself beyond delusion and the thought of separation is ceaseless bhakti.

✦

The Knowledge that is beyond forgetting and remembrance is ceaseless bhakti.

✦

That by which the Supreme is known, that by which the Guru is revealed, and that by which the Self is realized is ceaseless bhakti.

✦

That in which happiness is full, in which there is no return to illusion, in which peace is perfect and freedom is complete, in which love shines resplendently at its apex, and in which Self-Knowledge is self-evident is ceaseless bhakti.

✦

The inextinguishable lamp of divine love by which the darkness and gloom of delusion are rendered nonexistent is ceaseless bhakti.

✦

The devotion that illuminates perpetually, like a sun ever risen, and is of the nature of pure Consciousness is ceaseless bhakti.

✦

The devotion that reveals immortal Being as the only Self, in which all identity is absorbed, is ceaseless bhakti.

✦

The call of the eternal to itself is ceaseless bhakti, and the answer to this call is ceaseless bhakti.

✦

Parabhakti is timeless.

✦

In the Temple of Being,
The Space of Consciousness,

ॐ श्री रमणार्पणमस्तु

om śrī ramaṇārpaṇamastu

Om. May this be an offering to
Sri Ramana

✦

Chapter VI

Continuous absorption in the undivided Supreme One, yet with engagement in particular, focused, devotional practices, is a practice of bhakti.

✦

Reciting and singing the names of God, understanding their meaning and absorbed in the named, the nameless One, is a practice of bhakti.

✦

Remembrance and expression of devotion to God or the Guru, immersed in the ineffable, glorious, spiritual joy of God or the Guru, who is beyond thought, forgetfulness and remembrance, is a practice of bhakti.

✦

Gazing upon the sanctified form of the Supreme, as Deity or Guru, perceiving the invisible with the vision of devotion, is a practice of bhakti.

✦

Going to the temple to worship, meditate upon, and realize the infinite One is a practice of bhakti.

✦

Service to the Guru, the temple, and to one's fellow beings, aware of the Grace, sacred purpose, and true Self, respectively, is a practice of bhakti.

✦

Puja performed for the purpose of worship, filled with devotion and with the mind entirely focused on the worshiped, the undifferentiated One, is a practice of bhakti.

✦

Attending satsang, knowing the invaluable nature of association with Being and that those who have realized the Truth are the Truth, is a practice of bhakti.

✦

In the knowledge of the omnipresence and omnipotence of the Supreme, contemplation upon the truth that God is, God always is, and, wherever one may be, God is present is a practice of bhakti.

✦

Meditation, in which the separate identity
of the one who meditates dissolves and
delusive ideas are abandoned, upon the
inconceivable One by the devotion of
identity, is a practice of bhakti.

✦

Preservation of the spiritual teachings
inwardly and manifestly is a practice
of bhakti.

✦

Any activity engaged in with the divine
as the aim that leaves no scope for the
ego, free of the notions of "I" and "mine,"
becomes a practice of bhakti.

✦

Beyond the conception of practices and
one who practices is parabhakti.

✦

In the Temple of Being,
The Space of Consciousness,

ॐ श्री रमणार्पणमस्तु

om śrī ramaṇārpaṇamastu

Om. May this be an offering to
Sri Ramana

✦

Chapter VII

Ignorance vanishes, illusion dissolves,
bondage is removed, and suffering ends.
Such is the power of bhakti.

✦

True Knowledge becomes one's own and
self-evident. Such is the light of bhakti.

✦

Abidance in imperishable peace, full of
bliss, shines as direct experience. Such is
the result of bhakti.

✦

The way becomes clear, the path is followed free of deviation, the spiritual instruction is comprehended, the capacity to realize is manifested, and the goal, which is perfection, is found to be of the very nature of the ever-existent Self. Such is the magnificence of bhakti.

✦

All differences disappear, all doubts are removed, all sorrows are overcome, all fears dissipate, all desires are fulfilled, and even death loses its grief. Such is the promise of bhakti.

✦

Life's purpose is attained, the serenity of Reality is found, true Being is revealed, and the eternal remains. Such is the realization of bhakti.

✦

The Self alone exists and is real; this is ever so, this is ever so. Self-known is parabhakti.

In the Temple of Being,
The Space of Consciousness,

ॐ श्री रमणार्पणमस्तु

om śrī ramaṇārpaṇamastu

Om. May this be an offering to
Sri Ramana

PARABHAKTI
PART II

Chapter I

NAMAH SIVAYA

Om Namah Sivaya.

The words true,
Say Namah Sivaya.

The melody sublime,
Sing Namah Sivaya.

Deep in the mind,
Contemplate Namah Sivaya.

Absorbed in That,
Meditate on Namah Sivaya.

As That alone,
Abide as Namah Sivaya.

Fill the earth with the fragrance of
Namah Sivaya.

*Pour forth the water with the taste of
Namah Sivaya.*

*See the fire with the luminous eye of
Namah Sivaya.*

*The air full of the touch of
Namah Sivaya.*

*The pervasive space resounding with
Namah Sivaya.*

*From patala to satya,
Namah Sivaya.*

*From sristi (creation) to anugraha (grace),
Namah Sivaya.*

*From jagrat (waking) to turiya (the
fourth), and beyond,
Namah Sivaya.*

*From sravana (listening) to samadhi,
Namah Sivaya.*

*From "Who am I?" to "Sivo'ham,"
Namah Sivaya.*

*God, the Supreme Lord,
Namah Sivaya.*

The wonderful Sadguru,
Namah Sivaya.

The one Self of all,
Namah Sivaya.

The Self without all,
Namah Sivaya.

The one Reality,
Namah Sivaya.

Om Namah Sivaya.

✦

Chapter II

IN PRAISE OF THE ONE LIKE SPACE

1.

In which the entire universe appears,

In which it vanishes completely,

To the One who is like space

Salutation upon salutation,
again and again.

2.

In which the body appears, along with
the senses,

In which they dissolve, inevitably so,

To the One who is like space

Salutation upon salutation,
again and again.

3.

In which the mind appears, with all
of its thoughts,

In which it vanishes, without a trace,

To the One who is like space

Salutation upon salutation,
again and again.

4.

The innermost, devoid of directions,

The One to be reached by devoted
Knowledge alone,

To the One who is like space

Salutation upon salutation,
again and again.

5.

In which deep sleep, dream, and
waking appear,

Which, itself, sleeps, dreams, and
wakes not,

To the One who is like space

Salutation upon salutation,
again and again.

6.

The One who is endless and without
beginning,

The eternal in which appears time, yet
is timeless,

To the One who is like space

Salutation upon salutation,
again and again.

7.

*The indivisible One undefined
by distance,*

*The immeasurable One with
no separation,*

To the One who is like space

*Salutation upon salutation,
again and again.*

8.

Containing all, which are only itself,

*All-pervading with nothing different
to pervade,*

To the One who is like space

*Salutation upon salutation,
again and again.*

9.

Illimitable, partless, boundless, and full,

Infinite, eternal, perfect, and changeless,

To the One who is like space

Salutation upon salutation,
again and again.

10.
The One who shines as pure
Consciousness,

The One who exists as Being alone,

To the One who is like space

Salutation upon salutation,
again and again.

11.
As space in space is only space,

Immutably undifferentiated is the Reality;

To the One who is like space

Salutation upon salutation,
again and again.

✦

In the Temple of Being

The Space of Consciousness

✦

Chapter III

REALIZE THE ONE
LIKE SPACE

1.

Can a corner be in space,

In the edgeless, the limitless?

To the egoless One this salutation,

Realize the One like space.

2.

Can paint be applied to color space

Or adhere to it at all?

To the undefined One this salutation,

Realize the One like space.

3.

What form can be attributed to space,

To the invisible, without attributes?

To the formless One this salutation,

Realize the One like space.

4.

Is there a place where space is not,

*The pervasive in which everywhere
appears?*

To the omnipresent One this salutation,

Realize the One like space.

5.

When a pot moves, does space move,

Which is within and all around?

To the immovable One this salutation,

Realize the One like space.

6.

When the pot shatters, does space break,

Unformed and indestructible?

To the immortal One this salutation,

Realize the One like space.

7.

*Is the room-space distinct from
that without,*

The space without a difference?

To the undivided One this salutation,

Realize the One like space.

8.

Can space be grasped by the hand,

The actionless, intangible?

To the sense-transcendent One
this salutation,

Realize the One like space.

9.

Can space be more or less anywhere,

Expansive and invariable?

To the infinite One this salutation,

Realize the One like space.

10.

What is like space, yet is not space,

From which space is not apart?

To the Differenceless this salutation,

Realize the One like space.

53

*For whom is space? Who knows
the space?*

The Consciousness supreme.

To eternal Being this salutation,

Realized as the One like space.

✦

In the Temple of Being

The Space of Consciousness

✦

Chapter IV

SPACE OF GRACE

1.

The perfect fullness undiminished,

Being without another,

The immense bliss, which is forever,

Of the One like space, the Grace.

2.

Ever present, everywhere,

Containing and pervasive,

Never lost, imperishable,

Of the One like space, the Grace.

3.

By One alone, all appears,

By One alone, all is sustained,

By One alone, all dissolves,

Of the One like space, the Grace.

4.

Unborn Lord of all those born,

Immortal God surviving death,

The clarity, tranquility,

Of the One like space, the Grace.

5.

For those confused, perplexed, in fear;

Granting complete peace,

The peerless power, luminous,

Of the One like space, the Grace.

6.

The light by which one meditates,

Saving response before the prayer,

Accomplishing all, ever shining,

Of the One like space, the Grace.

7.

Because of which devotion surges,

Due to which Knowledge is known,

Absorbing all, the utter Oneness,

Of the One like space, the Grace.

8.

That from which one cannot move,

Indeed, one's very Self,

None can cause the disappearance,

Of the One like space, the Grace.

9.

Caring divinely for all beings,

Whether recognized or not,

Carrying all, disturbed by none,

Of the One like space, the Grace.

10.

Incomparable, immeasurable,

Ineffable, true Being,

Consciousness in its own nature,

Of the One like space, the Grace.

11.

The perfect fullness never ending,

Repose, silent and serene,

Bestowing the blessing endless,

Of the One like space, the Grace.

✦

In the Temple of Being
The Space of Consciousness

✦

Chapter V

WITHIN THE ONE
LIKE SPACE

1.

Ever present everywhere,

The One like space is worshiped,

Upon the space-like One one meditates,

Within the One like space.

2.

Filled with space, a vessel moves,

The space within moves not,

*So, when the body moves, the Self
does not,*

The One within like space.

3.

The vessel created, the space not so,

The vessel destroyed, the space is not,

Without a beginning or an end,

Within the One like space.

4.

The space within, the space without,

No difference is there of the space,

Pervading entirely all forever,

The One within like space.

5.

Containing all, binding none,

Embracing all, untouched by any,

In which all are, which none can grasp,

Within the One like space.

6.

Space of the cave, deep within,

Space of the temple, shining, divine,

Space of the sky, with no limit,

Within the One like space.

7.

Itself unseen in which all see,

The seer's nature alone is seen,

Transparent, vast, immeasurable,

The One within like space.

8.

As space emptied into space,

Is only changeless space,

So the "I" and the Self,

The One within like space.

9.

Space in space is only space,

Undivided Being,

The one who realizes, the One realized,

The One within like space.

10.

Within the One like space,

Is solely One within like space;

The One within like space is always

Within the One like space.

11.

The space of God,

The space of the Guru,

The space of the Self,

The One within like space.

✦

In the Temple of Being
The Space of Consciousness

✦

Chapter VI

GRACIOUS INQUIRY

Absorb me in your grace;
Yet who am I that could be distinct
therefrom?

Dissolve me in your grace;
Yet who am I that could come forth
from you?

Merge with me in your grace;
Yet who am I that could be apart
therefrom?

Liberate me with your grace;
Yet who am I that could bind myself?

Save me with your grace;
Yet who am I that could be lost?

Rescue me with your grace;
Yet who am I that could be in peril?

Illumine me with your grace;
Yet who am I that could know darkness?

Uplift me with your grace;
Yet who am I to sink or fall?

Reveal yourself to me by your grace;
Yet who am I that would see or not?

Your grace it is the ability to inquire;
Yet who am I to realize or not?

Your grace, the Reality, alone ever is;
Who am I to imagine otherwise?

✦

Salutations to Siva.

Salutations to Dakshinamurti.

Salutations to Ribhu.

Salutations to Gaudapada Mahanta.

Salutations to Adi Sankara Acarya.

Salutations to Bhagavan
Sri Ramana Maharshi.

Salutations to all of the Knowers of
Truth, the Gurus of Self-Knowledge.

Salutations to Brahman, the eternal,
perfect fullness.

✦

In the Temple of Being,
The Space of Consciousness,

ॐ श्री रमणार्पणमस्तु
ॐ ब्रह्मज्ञानिभ्योऽर्पणमस्तु

om śrī ramaṇārpaṇamastu
om brahmajñānibhyo'rpaṇamastu

Om. May this be an offering to
Sri Ramana
Om. May this be an offering to the
Knowers of Brahman

✦

Other SAT Publications available are:

~The Song of Ribhu (The English Translation of The Tamil Ribhu Gita)

~The Ribhu Gita (The English Translation of The Sanskrit Ribhu Gita)

~A Bouquet of Nondual Texts

~Origin of Spiritual Instruction

~Essence of Enquiry

~Self-Knowledge

~Self-Realization

~Timeless Presence

~Svatmanirupanam, The True Definition of One's Own Self

~The Four Requisites for Realization and Self-Inquiry

~Nirvana Satkam, Six Verses on Nirvana

~Nirguna Manasa Puja, Worship of the Attributeless One in the Mind

~Saddarsanam and An Inquiry into the Revelation of Truth and Oneself

~Advaita Devatam, God of Nonduality

~The Essence of the Spiritual Instruction

~The Quintessence of True Being

~Ever Yours in Truth, Nome

~One Self

For other books on Advaita Vedanta and the Teachings of Sri Ramana Maharshi, please visit the SAT Temple website at: www.SATRamana.org

SAT

SOCIETY OF ABIDANCE IN TRUTH
1834 OCEAN STREET, SANTA CRUZ,
CALIFORNIA 95060
(831) 425-7287 ~ www.SATRamana.org
sat@cruzio.com

Printed in Great Britain
by Amazon